UNLIMITED WEALTH

*Understanding How-to Create
Multiple Sources of Income*

**WRITTEN BY
RYAN JAUNZEMIS**

UNLIMITED WEALTH:
Copyright © 2016 by Ryan Jaunzemis

ALL RIGHTS RESERVED.

The photos, images, & illustrations within this book
have either been provided by the author himself,
or have been given to the author
with the express written-permission for use within this book
from either the sole owner/individual, or the entity itself expressed.

No part of this book may be used/reproduced (etc.)
in any manner what-so-ever,
without the express written-permission from the author himself.

UNLIMITED WEATH
ISPN: 978-1537278414

Written by Ryan Jaunzemis.

Cover design by Ryan Jaunzemis.

DISCLAIMER

THE AUTHOR OF THIS BOOK (RYAN JAUNZEMIS) DOES NOT ASSUME ANY LIABILITY FOR YOUR PERSONAL ACTIONS.

The information in which I am going to be delivering to you here, within the pages/confines of this book, **MUST** be taken **FOR ENTERTAINMENT PURPOSES ONLY**!

If, **YOU THE READER**, so choose to partake in **ANY** of the following advice/activities discussed/suggested here within, then you do so, **AT YOUR OWN RISK**!

Upon reading this article, if you so choose to partake in **ANY** of the activities so mentioned, then you agree to waive the right to sue Ryan Jaunzemis, **AND, ANY OTHER APPLICABLE PARTIES,** and **ASSUME & ACCEPT ALL RISKS** arising from such activities. (*For example, such risks may include: Money laundering and/or tax evasion, etc; i.e.-using the specific techniques described here-within to earn mass-amounts of income but failing to perform the prior/proper legal precautions; such as applying-for/paying/filing the expected taxes on any such earned/unclaimed income, and then being sued by the IRS—etc-etc-etc.)

NOTE: Absolutely none of the tips/techniques described here-within are illegal, but some legal action can/will be taken against an individual if he/she fails to implicate the proper legal precautions beforehand.

Any such financial advice that is given here within, are reports of **MY OWN PERSONAL FINDINGS & EXPERIENCE**, and, is advice that **I MYSELF** have used within my own life, to which I have found to be most beneficial to **MY OWN** personal success, happiness, well-being, etc-etc. Any such advice given here within **MUST** be taken solely **FOR ENTERTAINMENT PURPOSES ONLY**, and, **AT YOUR OWN RISK**!

If, **YOU THE READER**, so choose to partake in **ANY** of the advice given here within, then **YOU THE PARTICIPANT, AGREES TO TAKE FULL RESPONSIBILITY FOR THEMSELVES, AND FOR THEIR ACTIONS**!

*REMEMBER: Before using any such advice, always remember to first consult your personal financial councilor/consultant, and always remember to take any/all the proper legal precautions beforehand.

"Success is not something that just happens when you do 1 or 2 "special" things. Success is something that EMERGES when an individual is implementing MANY different elements/aspects all at once."

-RYAN JAUNZEMIS, "10 STEPS TO SUCCESS"

TABLE OF CONTENTS

Disclaimer - 3

Quote - 5

Table of Contents - 7

Preface - 9

Multiple Sources of Income - 15

How-to Create a Vision Board - 35

Final Thoughts - 45

A Letter from Ryan - 49

About the Author - 51

Contact Information - 53

Extras - 55

PREFACE

10 years ago, after a very violent divorce, I arrived in the city of Las Vegas, broke, alone, depressed, and even suicidal.

I had recently lost my home, all of my worldly possessions (including my $200k recording studio; which I had spent a life time acquiring), but also, most importantly, I had lost access to both of my children.

After several misallegations in court, I was permanently barred from my place of residence by the New Castle Upon Tyne city council, and later (after violating my terms-of-probation), was ultimately banned from the United Kingdom! —Subject to ARREST upon reentry!

Upon arriving in the city of Las Vegas, I soon discovered the self-help section in the Barns & Noble bookstore, and began voraciously consuming books within the various topics of health, wealth, & relationship advice.

My initial goal—at first—was simply to begin rebuilding/reestablishing my life, possibly getting into a bit better shape, and hopefully getting a girlfriend.

Many of my new friends in which I had most recently met, had told me, quote-unquote, that all of this self-help stuff in which I had been studying was just, "mumbo-jumbo"; though I relentlessly continued studying, and soon, began to put many of these new tips & techniques in which I had learned into practice.

Shortly thereafter, I had soon discovered a secret underground society known as, "The Seduction Community" (or, The PUA Community; i.e.-Pick-up Artist Community); an international organization of men who traded tips & techniques on how-to seduce women. Upon discovering this information, I quickly spent over $3k of my own money on some of this new material, learned it, and then put it into action.

In a very short time, I had ended up dating several hundred different women—many of them being extremely beautiful women; exotic dancers, go-go dancers, restaurant hostesses, and even porn stars!

My friends were absolutely astonished, and wanted to learn these new secret techniques in which I was using themselves. I soon begin crafting out simple (yet effective) Power Point presentations in order to teach other guys these techniques.

In a very short time I had ended up becoming the #1 dating & relationship coach in Las Vegas, and was later featured on the covers of both Las Vegas' SEVEN & CITY LIFE Magazines! I then later went on a 22-city tour across America where I was able to then teach these same techniques to 100s-of-thousands of different single men & women.

Simultaneously, while all of this was happening, I was also studying & reading through several other self-help books on the various topics of health & fitness, diet & nutrition, and also, financial & wealth-building advice.

Before I had started out I was approximately 225 pounds, but, after applying several of these health & fitness techniques in which I had learned, within just a few short months of training I was now weighing-in at 160 pounds, and was now staring back at myself in the mirror seeing my new rock-solid 6-pack abs! —It was absolutely INCREDIBLE! —And, the women to whom I was dating at the time were absolutely loving it!

What happened next was nothing short of AMAZING! Many of my new dating coaching clients, because I was now charging upwards of $2,500.00 per day to work with me 1-on-1 (via private coaching), and, was also doing huge seminars & group workshops, many of the clientele in which I was attracting, were extremely financially successful business men, but simply had no GAME (or confidence, etc.) when it came to approaching women. But, interestingly enough, these men were all very well established/connected within several other secret societies/organizations (etc.), and, had begun to invite me along with them to some of these secret underground meetings in which were being hosted by some very elite members of society; many in which I am not legally allowed to name publicly.

I began attending these secret meetings where I learned several secret techniques—directly from the super-rich & super-wealthy—about how-to quickly create & establish what was described as, "unlimited levels of wealth & abundance" in my life. One of these techniques being—which I will be describing within this book in greater detail—a technique known as: "***Multiple Sources of Income***." This is a technique in which a person may use in order to begin earning what is known as, "***passive income***." (*Which I will describe later.)

The most amazing thing is that: **ANYONE CAN DO THIS!** It requires no special skill at all! —And, I will explain exactly HOW it is accomplished.

And so, after 10 long years of research—and also, from going from broke, to earning mass-amounts of income—I present to you, this extremely quick & easy guide, of how YOU TOO can now begin implementing this very simple strategy, and quickly begin earning more money than you may have ever thought possible!

I hope that this book will help you to achieve all of your wildest dreams. May unlimited wealth, abundance, & prosperity find you. Good luck!

Your friend,

Ryan Jaunzemis
www.RyanJaunzemisLifestyleCoaching.com | 702.417.7714

MULTIPLE SOURCES
OF INCOME

I'd like to first ask you a few questions: **Are you ready to start achieving UNLIMITED-LEVELS of WEALTH & ABUNDANCE in your life? Are you ready to learn one of the most HEAVILY-GUARDED, HIGHLY TOP-SECRET, WEALTH-BUILDING STRATEGIES/TECHNIQUES directly from the super-rich, & super-elite?** Take just a few moments to ponder on these questions.

You see, most people have the fundamental established idea (as programmed into them by society), that in order to attract MORE wealth/abundance into

UNLIMITED WEALTH

their lives, that they must do either 1 of 2 things: 1, they must either WORK MORE HOURS. Or 2, they must get a 2nd/3rd/4th job, etc-etc-etc. Fair? Well, I believe that BOTH of these two options are LOSING STRATEGIES for attracting more wealth/abundance into your life.

If we take a deeper look into how money can be made, we will clearly see that there are three (3) VERY distinct ways of earning it.

These three (3) ways being:

(1) Trading TIME for money (i.e.-working an hourly/salary position for an employer).

(2) Investing/gambling (i.e.-using previously-earned/borrowed-money to either use to: 1, invest within the HOPES that it MAY garner/generate MORE revenues. Or, 2, gamble, and/or bet with it; in the mere HOPES that you may ultimately win MORE MONEY back in return).

Or, finally **(3)**, you can make money from what many wealthy people out there would describe as, "*multiple-sources of income*" (*also known as **diversity/diversive-income/diversification/passive-income, etc**; along with several other such names); i.e.-creating one (1) or more sources/products, etc, in which are readily available, and are for sale to the public. (*which is what we are going to discuss here in greater detail.) (**Also, for more information on creating *multiple sources of income*, and for many other strategies for creating more wealth, success, &**

abundance in your life, make sure to check out my new #1 bestselling book: "10 STEPS TO SUCCESS"; available in paperback & Kindle on Amazon.com)

If you take a closer look at the more wealthier people within our society you will quickly come to discover that most of them are earning their money via *multiple-sources of income*.

Most people tend to think that in order to earn MORE MONEY that they will thus then have to start working 2 or more jobs, and start working 80+ hours per week... or, perhaps try to work some OVER-TIME so as to try and earn TIME-AND-A-HALF. Do any of these situations sound familiar to you?

UNLIMITED WEALTH

The problem here, is that even if a person were to work 100+ hours per week, this individual will still be having to trade their TIME in exchange for MONEY, and (also), there will ultimately still be a SALARY-CAP in position on this specific individual's income—which is what I'm going to assume that you do NOT want. Fair?

I believe that if YOU are like MOST people, then what YOU are probably REALLY wanting, is to have MORE MONEY, and also, to have MORE FREE TIME! —Sounds pretty good, right?

Well, a few years back, during several secret underground business & marketing meetings/conferences in which I had the pleasure of attending with some very elite members of society, I had quickly stumbled upon this new idea, and had realized, that in order to start making MORE MONEY (and also to be able to have MORE FREE TIME; so as to pursue many of my other dreams, goals, passions, & desires, etc-etc-etc), that I would have to begin creating what these various wealthy people—in whom I had been introduced to—had described as "*multiple-sources of income*" for myself.

I had realized that I had ALREADY recently developed SEVERAL things (i.e.-products) within my own life, in which I could possibly/potentially be earning income from (i.e.-*passive income*); but, at the time, I had not yet put 2-and-2-together.

To give you a brief bit of history, in my personal life I have been making music since I was 4-years-old. Over the course of the last 30+ years I have roughly created over 15,000+ songs (*though several-thousand of these works were destroyed during a major power-outage back in 2003 in which had deleted my entire computer hard-drive; though I still had several-thousand others saved/remaining on an alternate hard drive).

I had quickly come to realize that each of these songs (in this new digital, self-publishing world in which we now reside in), could potentially EACH be sold as a "single" on iTunes for 99¢ (*or $1.29, or $2.00—etc-etc-etc), or, even an entire album for $9.98 (*or $11.99, or $17.99—etc-etc-etc), right?

Basically, the bottom-line is this: **The more products in which a business puts out, the more potential income/revenue one can theoretically be earning!**

UNLIMITED WEALTH

Makes sense, right? To put this more bluntly, each single product in which a person/business puts out there can thus be considered **ANOTHER** *multiple-source of income*! Make sense?

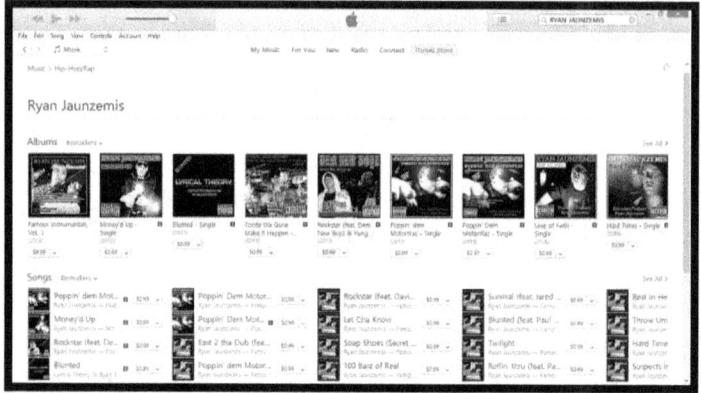

For example, back in 1997 I was a professional rollerblader (aggressive in-line skater), and soon became sponsored by a skate shoe company called "Soap Shoes." I later became one of the poster boys for this company, was featured in their commercials which played internationally, went of tour with them, and later, had wrote an autobiography about my ventures of becoming the #1 Soaper in the world entitled, "**SOAP SHOES** — *Secret Tips & Tricks*" (which is currently available for sale on Amazon.com).

Now, here's the technique in action: This single book/product ALONE is one (1) source of my income.

This means that whenever a person/customer/reader, etc, buys one (1) or more copies of this book/product, the royalties which are earned are then INSTANTLY deposited into my bank/PayPal account, etc, and will thus then be readily available to me for spending! This means that I can essentially be making money WHILE I SLEEP! —Sounds pretty cool, right?

Think about this for just a moment: The product is DONE… COMPLETE… FINISHED! I never, ever, EVER have to touch it again!

Now, for THAT one (1) specific body-of-work I did spend approximately 18+ months of my life (and all of my free-time, etc), writing & editing it, and then finally getting it published, but, now… it's ABSOLUTELY FINISHED! —And, is thus now being hosted online via a 3rd-party manufacturer/distributor. This means that personally, I never even have to look at this product again if I don't feel like it! —It's done! This

UNLIMITED WEALTH

means that I can be on vacation in the tropics, relaxing somewhere in a hammock on a peaceful deserted white-sandy beach, and I can STILL potentially be making money! —Just imagine the possibilities!

For example, perhaps some skater kid in Croatia (or the Netherlands, or France, or Guam, or New Delhi— or ANYWHERE ELSE on the planet!) may be perusing around online, and, who just happens to like Soap Shoes, and then, just decides to pull out their parent's credit card and purchase my product.

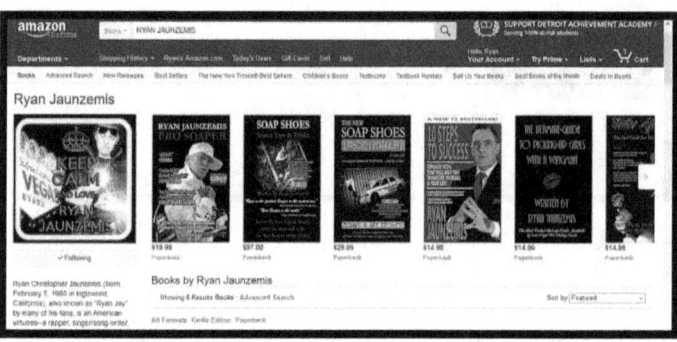

So again, this means that I can be dozing-off in some relaxing hammock, strung-out between two palm trees out in the tropics, and then… "DING!" Get an alert/notification on my iPhone (as obviously if I was relaxing in a hammock out in the tropics then you could probably guess that my iPhone would most likely be set on vibrate, or left back in my hotel room on the charge, etc), which will quickly inform me that MONEY has just been deposited into my bank/PayPal account, etc! —How amazing is that? This means no more 9-5-job slaving away for someone else! —No boss! No stupid time-card having to clock-in & out! No having to deal with customers! No ass-kissing! No hassle! No bull-shit! No NOTHING!

Now, here's the kicker! —And, THIS is how you're going to make that REAL money! It has been found that anytime a person creates a body-of-work, it can instantly be split into three (3) OR MORE SEPARATE SOURCES OF INCOME!

For example, if I were to record a piece-of-information in video format, then I would now have a VIDEO for sale, correct? (i.e.-a video information product.) But, if we were to then strip the video (i.e.-the visual portion), then what now would we then be left with? Well, we would then still be left with the AUDIO portion of this product. This portion of the product can then me manufactured into CD/.MP3/.WAV-file/.AIFF format—etc-etc-etc) which we can then ALSO sell! This means that we now have two (2) separate products, correct? (A **VIDEO** product, and an **AUDIO** product!)

Now, what if we then strip the audio portion of this product? What would we then be left with? Well, we would then still be left with a **TEXT** version of whatever happened to have been said on this video/audio file (etc); which can thus then either be sold as a **Kindle** (i.e.-E-book/.PDF file, etc), and, also, a **PAPERBACK** version (*which when a physical paper-product is made, it then too can ALSO be split between not only a paperback version, but also, a **HARDCOVER** version, etc; i.e.-two (2) separate products yet again!

So, in the end: One (1) single video-information-product (***VSL***, for example) has now thus become sellable as now **FIVE (5) SEPARATE PRODUCTS!** —All of which can potentially be making a person money WHILE THEY SLEEP!

ALTERNATE FORMATS

So, why create different formats of the same thing? Well, you see, different people enjoy DIFFERENT TYPES of media—plain & simple! —And also, most importantly, from a business & marketing stand-point: **PROVEN!** And, to take this concept even further, some people also enjoy **COLLECTIONS**, and/or ALL FORMS of any PARTICULAR PERSON(s)/ARTIST(s)/AUTHOR(s) work—etc.

For example, Erik Von Markovic is one of my personal favorite authors. He has a dating & seduction book entitled, "**The Mystery Method**" which I absolutely LOVE! —And, to which I continue to read, & re-read, all the time! But, I don't just own the paperback version of this book, I also own the audio book version of it as well—so that I can listen to it in my car on the way to work, or when I am jogging on my treadmill, etc. Plus, I ALSO own the Kindle E-Book version of this product as well—so that I can read it on my iPhone during my breaks if I am perhaps out-and-about—etc.

So, even though this product might be the SAME PRODUCT, when it is split into various different forms of media, the author/producer/artist, etc-etc, can also be getting paid in MULTIPLE WAYS! Make sense?

In the case of the previous example, I have personally paid this particular author three (3) separate times! (*Even though it was essentially for the exact SAME PRODUCT!) And, myself, along with several other highly successful individuals, in which I personally happen to know, all do the exact same thing—with MANY different products!

Perhaps YOU may have even done this to some extent within your own life without even knowing it? Try looking around your house to see if YOU have bought a particular author(s)/artist(s) work in multiple formats. Perhaps a paperback book & audio book of the same title?

For example, my new book, "**10 STEPS TO SUCCESS**" is available in paperback, but, it is also available in a Kindle/E-book version, and, it is also available as a streamable audio-version on my YouTube channel as well! What is interesting here, is that I STILL get paid even though the streamable audio version is available for FREE on YouTube, and also, on my website: www.RyanJaunzemisLifestyleCoaching.com as well, because I am a YouTube Partner and my YouTube channel is MONETIZED! This means that any video in which a person watches on my YouTube channel will have ads running across it periodically. This means that if an ad is displayed (*and then clicked upon by a viewer), then I get paid! This money just racks-up in a special "YouTube account" and I am then sent a check in the mail periodically from YouTube every time I hit a specific monetary threshold! This means that even though a person might be reading my **10 STEPS TO SUCCESS** book (or listening to it, etc) it is not just one (1) single product, it is actually—at minimum—three (3) DIFFERENT products (*or more) in one! Make sense?

In my book, "**SOAP SHOES — *Secret Tips & Tricks***" this is not just one (1) single book/product either! The full product is the quote-on-quote "full-color, deluxe, paperback version"; which is available for

$97.00 dollars on Amazon.com. But, as you may guess, not everyone out there may be able to afford $97.00, fair? This being the case, I have also made a more affordable, "black & white version" entitled, "**PRO SOAPER**"; which is also available in paperback for $19.95, and on Kindle as an E-book for $2.99. I have also extracted only certain/specific parts of this particular product and have used these extractions in order to create entirely new products; which are known within the publishing world as: "**EXCERPTS**." (***Such as this book, "UNLIMITED WEALTH"; which is an excerpt from my book, "10 STEPS TO SUCCESS."**)

For example, my book "**THE NEW SOAP SHOES TRICKTIONARY (*Version 2.0*)**" is actually PART-

UNLIMITED WEALTH

OF my book "**SOAP SHOES —** *Secret Tips & Tricks*", but, what if perhaps someone ONLY wants to learn the actual Soap Shoe's tricks, but is not necessarily interested in reading my personal story/autobiography, etc, or any of the other add-ins? (Etc.) Well, the solution was to create an **excerpt**; which is now an entirely new source of income! (1) A **paperback** book. (2) An **E-book**. (3) An **audio-book**! Does this make sense?

The lesson here, is that you can strip one (1) single product into as many different separate sources of income as you want and continue capitalizing your income! **You can take this as far as you want to go!**

The New Soap Shoes Tricktionary Version 2.0
by Ryan C Jaunzemis
Paperback
$26.96 $29.95 ✓*Prime*
Get it by **Tuesday, Sep 1**
FREE Shipping on orders over $35
12 offers from $22.96
1 Other Format: Kindle Edition $2.99

Now, just imagine if you were to create an entire product-line/product-curriculum, etc-etc, for your personal business (i.e.-books, CDs, .mp3s, DVDs, instant downloads, etc-etc-etc-etc-etc! Imagine all of the money in which you could then potentially be earning via *multiple sources of income*, rather than slaving away at some 9-5 desk job in which you most likely hate?

TAKE A YEAR OFF!

I would urge you to try and take off possibly the next 1-2 years from your life, so as to begin to spend all of your free-time creating your new *multiple sources of income*!

A year from now, you could potentially be making money WHILE YOU SLEEP while all of your other friends are still out there grinding away, and working

UNLIMITED WEALTH

their same old, boring, 9-5, dead-end jobs! —This is the REAL secret to attracting more wealth & abundance into your life, and generating mass-amounts of income very quickly, & efficiently!

This is the time for it guys! With 3rd-party manufactures/distributors available at the click of a mouse... with the rise of the internet... with the rise of social media and other online stores & publishing companies (etc), this is now the time to make it happen!

Also, you will begin to notice that as the more products in which you release, the more people will begin to watch your YouTube videos; which means more money for more clicks on more ads! (Etc.) But, also, as more people watch your videos, more people will also thus begin visiting your website(s) and begin purchasing more of your products; which means (again) MORE MONEY from more product SALES! In time, you will soon notice, that everything in which you are doing will soon begin to compound upon itself! —Very similar to the effect of an AVALANCHE!

It may take you some time in order to find the right hill, and ball-up together your snowball of success. But, as you slowly begin to ball this snowball together, and begin slowly rolling it through the snow and down the hill, sooner-or-later, as you get a solid enough ball together, and it begins to slowly—but surly—pick up speed & momentum as it rolls along down the hill, it will soon begin to grow EXPONENTIALLY bigger, and bigger, AND BIGGER! —And so on and so forth!

One (1) new product out there may start making you just a bit of extra grocery money. Five (5) new products out there may make you enough the following year to purchase a new home. Ten or twenty plus (10 or 20+), new products... plus your new DVD... plus your new clothing line... plus your new BLANK, and BLANK, and BLANK (etc-etc-etc-etc-etc). —You get the idea, right?

UNLIMITED WEALTH

For example, watch the way musicians/bands use this unique technique. Many of the top music artists in the world make records and sell CDs/.MP3 downloads, etc, but, they also play live shows & sell concert tickets.

The revenues from selling these concert tickets are one (1) of their *multiple sources of income*. They may also sell merchandise at their concerts, and also, on their websites; i.e.-T-shirts, hats, sweatshirts, etc-etc-etc-etc-etc (all of which would be considered *multiple source of income*). Some may even go as far as hiring a film crew so as to video tape their live concerts/performances/events, etc, and then sell this recording as a DVD or instant download for their fans as well! They may also make money off YouTube music videos, interviews, stories, documentaries, etc-etc-etc-etc-etc.

The reason most big name bands are so successful is that they don't necessarily focus on making one big "hit" like so many amateur garage-band musicians may dream of.

Successful bands more-so focus on building an ENTERPRISE of *multiple sources of income*—at least that's what I've picked-up along the way working with several-thousand of the top-name music acts within the music/entertainment industry. Make sense?

I would urge you to try this technique. Do it! Enjoy it! And begin to watch money start to flow towards you from all different angles!

UNLIMITED WEALTH

This technique can even be taken up a notch to, instead of putting out multiple products, maybe perhaps you might want to own multiple BUSINESSES; i.e.-fast food restaurant chains/franchises, apartment buildings/complexes, convenience stores, etc-etc-etc-etc-etc! —The possibilities are ENDLESS!

Have fun with this technique, and may you succeed in whatever it is that you wish to do!

For more information, and for more tips & tricks on attracting more wealth, abundance, & prosperity into your life, then make sure to pick-up a copy of my new book, "**10 STEPS TO SUCCESS**."

*Don't forget to **SUBSCRIBE** to my new YouTube channel: **www.YouTube.com/TheRyanJayShow**

Best of luck to you, and may you prosper greatly!

REMEMBER: *Multiple-sources of income*!

HOW-TO CREATE A VISION BOARD

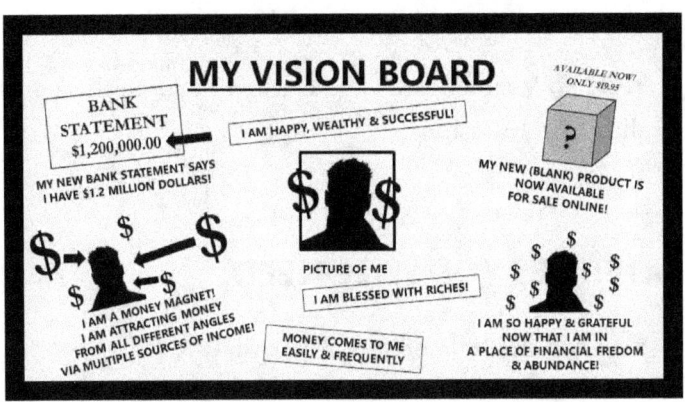

WHAT IS A "VISION BOARD?"

So, what is a vision board? A vision board (or dream board, etc) is typically a poster board on which one can use so as to glue/paste/tape/collage (etc-etc) various images in which one may have either printed/drawn, or torn out from various magazines—et cetera.

The idea behind this, is that when a person surrounds themselves with images of WHO they would like to become, WHAT exactly they want to have, WHERE they might like to live, or WHERE they might like to vacation (etc-etc-etc-etc-etc), they are then subconsciously re-programming their mind in order to begin making any/all life changes necessary in order to match these same images/dreams/desires, etc. By doing this, a person's brain (i.e.-more specifically, one's subconscious mind) will thus begin to proactively move the body into position so as to fulfill these desires.

NOTE: Vision boards add clarity to your desires, and feeling to your visions.

SUPPLIES YOU WILL NEED:

You will need: Poster/cork board, etc, magazines/pictures, scissors, glue (*not "Elmer's" glue; as it makes the pages ripple), rubber cement, tape, markers, stickers, etc-etc-etc.

HOW-TO MAKE A VISION BOARD

It is quite easy to create a vision board. I will explain the process in just six (6) easy steps:

Step #1:

First, you will want to find (and then begin to go through) various pictures & magazines, and then start cutting the images out from them.

NOTE: No gluing yet! Just enjoy yourself and have lots of fun looking through magazines, and cutting out various pictures/words/headlines, etc, in which strike your fancy.

Step #2:

Go through the images and begin to lay out your favorites on the board. Try to eliminate any/all images in which no longer *feel* right; this is where your intuition must come into play.

As you begin to lay out the pictures/images on your board, you may slowly get a sense of how the board SHOULD eventually be laid out.

For instance, you might assign a certain/specific THEME to each different corner, or place on the board. Or, it may just be that the images will seem to want to go all over the place.

NOTE: You can always reassess what you want later.

For example: Perhaps in the TOP-RIGHT corner of the board you may want to dedicate this space to what your first *multiple source of income* will be (or what perhaps it may look like, etc) by cutting out different pictures of different types of products in which you may what to create for yourself. While on the TOP-LEFT side of the board, you may want to dedicate this space

UNLIMITED WEALTH

to what you would envision your overall financial success to look like (etc).

Step #3:

Glue, tape, or tack down everything onto the board. You may want to begin adding in writing if you want. You can paint on it, or you can write words on it with markers.

REMEMBER: This is <u>YOUR</u> vision board! There are no rules in regards to doing it "right or wrong." These are <u>YOUR</u> private dreams & fantasies.

Step #4: (*Optional, but powerful.)

Leave space in the very center of your vision board for a fantastic photo of yourself where you look radiant & happy. Simply paste a picture of yourself directly in the center of your board. By doing this technique you will begin to view your board similar to that of a mirror.

When you begin waking up and looking at your vision board in the morning (during your *morning ritual*), and seeing your own face in the center surrounded with images of things such as money, or other symbols of financial freedom, abundance, prosperity, etc-etc-etc, your subconscious mind will quickly begin to move your body in such a fashion so as to physically manifest these desires. (*There is a scientifical explanation of exactly why this happens, but we do not have time to cover it in this book.)

Step #5:

Hang your vision board in a place where you will see it often; perhaps on a wall in your bedroom or directly above your bed (etc).

NOTE: If your vision board is not necessarily suitable/acceptable in the presence of company or other people (etc), for example, perhaps you dream of relaxing on vacation on a tropical beach with a huge wallet of brand-new, crisp, green, one hundred dollar bills and throwing them up in the air, while being surrounded with beautiful naked women, you can put these images on your vision board and then just simply hang your vision board inside of a walk in closet (if you have one), or any other such private place where it will not be seen in the presence of others. Make sense?

Step #6:

Stare into your vision board and try to BURN the images into your mind.

Look at your vision board for a few minutes each & every morning as you wake up (**only for about 10-15**

minutes or so), and then, begin to consciously ask yourself this question: **What can I start doing TODAY that is going to help assist me in accomplishing these goals?**

Also, try turning on your favorite piece of music, or lighting a few candles, and simply add this ritual into a normal part of your morning/evening routine.

NOTE: Enjoy your vision board, for it is the beginning of the unfolding of that in which you desire.

RAISING YOUR VIBRATION

Try and focus upon your new vision board with positive feelings & energy, and really try to *feel* the feelings of ALREADY having the money in which you want, or the goal/desire, etc.

Try to close your eyes and imagine these same images appearing on the scroll of your mind.

By thinking about these images throughout your day your brain will naturally bring you to new paramount realizations/ideas, etc, of things in which you might be able to do which may bring you closer to your dreams/goals/desires, etc. **If/when you receive any specific inspired thoughts make sure to write them down IMMEDIATELY, and then, ACT upon them!**

Try to remember, that when doing this exercise, to release any/all expectations about GETTING the money. **That is for another day, and another time!**

While you are doing this exercise, try to focus more solely upon the *FEELINGS* about what it would be like to already HAVE these *multiple sources of income* in place, and what it would be like to already be collecting/generating income—**as if you were ALREADY receiving it.**

The idea here, is that you become so engulfed within the IDEA of already having this new level of wealth & abundance, that the pain, urgency, & desperation of NOT having the levels of wealth in which you may want will soon be eliminated from your mind/aura/being/vibration, etc.

By re-programming your brain—by using your vision board so as to help you to start actually believing & experiencing the feelings of ALREADY having this new level of wealth & abundance—you will quickly eliminate any/all feelings of that of a lower vibration (such as sadness & depression, etc), and you will quickly replace them with feelings of that of a higher vibration (such as feelings of happiness, fulfillment, & elation, etc).

Day-by-day, little-by-little, you will begin shifting your reality from the one in which you are now presently living, into that of the new reality in which you are wanting.

DIFFERENT TYPES OF VISION BOARDS

There are several different types of vision boards that a person can make/construct, etc. You can make vision boards for things in which you want to buy, or goals in which you might like to achieve. You can make one specifically for the type of dream car/cars/vehicles, etc, that you want/desire, or you can make one about different vacation spots, or other places in which you might like to travel to (etc).

REMEMBER: Again, this is YOUR vision board! These boards/images/fantasies, etc, are for YOUR EYES ONLY! These are YOUR private fantasies. No one is judging you, or what you want/desire as a man. You have the right to have ANYTHING that you so desire in life, so remember: **ANYTHING goes!**

Have fun with this! Let your imagination run wild! Dream away about the financial success, abundance, &

prosperity in which you want. Again: **Have fun with this!**

ADDING AFFIRMATIONS & TAG LINES

After you fill up your vision board with cut-outs of pictures that you enjoy looking at, the next thing in which you are going to want to do, is to start adding-in positive *affirmations* & *tag lines*.

What I mean by adding-in words, *affirmations*, & *tag lines*, etc, is to begin adding-in words/phrases, etc, to really bring your images to life!

For example, if you have a picture of yourself surrounded with cold hard cash raining down all around you, then add in a *tag line* underneath this picture, one which might say something to the extent of: **I AM SO HAPPY & GRATEFUL NOW THAT I AM IN A PLACE OF FINANCIAL FREEDOM & ABUNDANCE!** —Or anything else in which you may feel directly resonates with YOU & YOUR VISION or YOUR FUTURE.

Remember that you can add ANYTHING that you want in these *tag lines*. You can even make them as speech bubbles as if, for example, you were to cut out a picture of one of your potential customers were talking to you; you can even talk right back to them, and have conversations with them if you want to!

REMEMBER: Don't be afraid to day dream & fantasize about your dreams/goals/desires (etc). This exercise may sound absolutely ridiculous, but Albert Einstein even once said: ***"Imagination is everything. It is the preview of life's coming attractions."*** Remember that!

NOTE: If you cannot find an EXACT picture that suits your vision, don't be afraid to sit-down and actually try to draw-out the image yourself.

FINAL THOUGHTS

Now, let's be realistic here. Most people will read this material, get all motivated & pumped-up, but will most likely never take the first ACTION-STEP in order to START creating their very FIRST *multiple source of income*. Others may read this material, and may quickly become overwhelmed as to the possible pressure, and quite possibly the TIME it may take to actually sit-down and create several different *multiple sources of income*. Well, let me give you a strategy in which I believe may help yield to you proven results.

First things first. You don't have to go as crazy, or as overboard as myself. I have literally dedicated years, & YEARS of my life to this process, and have also sacrificed almost everything I have in order to become the author of now over 50+ different books, and to create multiple audio & DVD programs (etc), for my various businesses. But, you don't need to take it THAT far if you don't want to.

The main idea/concept in which I am trying to teach you here, is that you can use this technique to help you to earn whatever salary you like!

You see, not everyone wants to me a multi-millionaire, or billionaire! Not everyone cares whether-or-not they are clearing 6-figures! These types of desires are only for

UNLIMITED WEALTH

certain types of people. Many may be surprised to hear me make a claim/statement such as this, but in reality it's actually true—and I will explain.

You see, there are many people out there who don't care whether-or-not they have millions of dollars. Many people may dream of such lavish/opulent lifestyles, etc, while many other people out there may dream simply to one day be able to retire from their job and live in a quiet log cabin up in the plush-green forests of Canada (for example) with their wife & children; relaxing with their feet up by their fireplace, and spending their days tending to their small herb garden in their backyard.

You see, we all want different things in life—and that's okay! Again, some people out there may dream of making millions of dollars, and you can definitely use the technique described in this book in order to create this type of level of wealth within your life, while other people out there would just be happy for a few hundred extra bucks in their pocket each month—and that's fine too! You can use this technique however you wish to!

If you enjoy your day job, but perhaps you would now like to, or have now become inspired to create one additional source of income; such as a published book, or possibly some new invention, or anything else along those lines (i.e.-anything yielding *passive income*), then by all means! —Make that your goal to do so!

Try to imagine things from this perspective: **If you can begin employing this technique, even to start bringing in an additional $100.00 per month, that's an extra $1,200.00 of unexpected/*passive income* per year! If you can start bringing in an extra $1000.00 per month, that's an extra $12,000.00 per year! —Et cetera!** Just imagine the possibilities!

Now, I understand that not everyone is going to have the necessary skill-set for writing/editing (etc) in order to write a book, or may have the necessary skill-set in order to film/edit (etc) a video program, or will have the skill-set necessary to record/mix/master (etc) an audio program, or have the necessary available funds needed in order to create a new invention, or file for the necessary patents for one (etc-etc-etc-etc-etc), and that's okay! You have to understand that these things WILL take time! —It is a process!

I am going to recommend to you—and I know that this may sound difficult at first, as you may still be working (or stuck at) your normal 9-5 job—that you try to set up a specific time everyday; as part of your normal daily routine/ritual, etc, in which you will be dedicating all of your POWER, FOCUS, & INTENT on creating your first new product. This is an entrepreneurial-technique known as creating "***focused blocks***" of time. (*I do discuss this technique MUCH further, and in MUCH greater detail in my new #1 bestselling book: "**10 STEPS TO SUCCESS**." I would DEFINITELY

UNLIMITED WEALTH

recommend to you that you check it out in the section under "*clean focus*.")

Again, this is not something that is going to just happen for you overnight. This is a process that is going to take time—and, in some cases... YEARS! —But, don't be discouraged! With hard work & dedication, YOU TOO may soon be literally making money while you sleep!

Good luck! I wish you all the best!

A LETTER FROM RYAN

Dear friend,

I want to personally thank you for purchasing my product. I hope that this book has brought you a few new insights, and, I hope that my advice will assist you in making more money, and achieving more success.

For more advice on attracting more wealth & abundance, make sure to visit my new website: www.RyanJaunzemisLifestyleCoaching.com

To your success, this is Ryan Jaunzemis. I wish you all the best!

Thank you, & best wishes to you all!

Your friend,

Ryan Jaunzemis
www.RyanJaunzemisLifestyleCoaching.com | 702.417.7714

ABOUT THE AUTHOR

Ryan Christopher Jaunzemis (Born February 5, 1980 in Inglewood, California), also known as "Ryan Jay" by many of his fans/followers, is an American born virtuoso; a rapper, singer/song-writer, executive-producer/director, professional athlete, professional in-line skater/Soaper, male model, bestselling author, master pick-up artist, lifestyle, dating, relationship, & self-help guru, internet marketer, photographer/videographer, graphic-designer, tattoo-artist, black-belt/martial-arts master, and recording/theatrical engineer.

Ryan is the chief organizer of The Las Vegas PUA Lair and has been rated the #1 dating coach in Las Vegas. He has recently been featured in several hundred

UNLIMITED WEALTH

different videos, websites, & internet publications, including: **Las Vegas' SEVEN & CITY LIFE Magazines**, **PUA Magazine**, **www.PUALingo.com**, **HER OBSESSION & OBSESSION SYSTEMS Magazines**, **VICE Media, The RIDE Channel**, **COMPLEX Sneakers Magazine**, **H3H3 Productions**, as well as several professional skating/Soaping videos & DVDs, and has now reached over 6M combined YouTube views.

Ryan is the author/producer of over 50+ different books, CDs, DVDs, and other publications, and is currently working on several new projects as well.

Ryan currently resides in Las Vegas, Nevada.

*For more information on Ryan Jaunzemis, please visit: www.RyanJaunzemisBiography.com

CONTACT INFORMATION

iPhone 6S:
(FaceTime, Skype, Tango, ooVoo, etc, available)
702.417.7714

E-MAIL
Ryan@RyanJaunzemisMusic.com

FACEBOOK
www.Facebook.com/RyanJaunzemis
www.Facebook.com/RyanJaunzemisLifestyleAndDatingCoachingPage

YOUTUBE
www.YouTube.com/TheRyanJayShow

INSTAGRAM
@jaunzemis

TWITTER
@ryanjaunzemis

SNAPCHAT
@jaunzemis

ALSO AVAILABLE BY THIS AUTHOR:

"10 STEPS TO SUCCESS"

WRITTEN BY
RYAN JAUNZEMIS

(Visit: www.Amazon.com for more details)

www.ingramcontent.com/pod-product-compliance
Lightning Source LLC
Chambersburg PA
CBHW070405190526
45169CB00003B/1122